At the Fire Station

by Victor Violi

PEARSON

Scott
Foresman

Editorial Offices: Glenview, Illinois • Parsippany, New Jersey • New York, New York
Sales Offices: Needham, Massachusetts • Duluth, Georgia • Glenview, Illinois
Coppell, Texas • Sacramento, California • Mesa, Arizona

helmet

fire fighters

fire hose

The fire fighters are on the job! They work as a team. Each fire fighter has a special job to do.

Some fire fighters drive the truck. Drivers must know how to drive the truck safely. They must know the quickest route to the fire. Drivers must watch out for cars and people.

---

route: way to get to a particular place

When they get to the fire, the fire fighters hop out of the truck. Some hurry to hook up the hose. They spray water on the fire.

Some fire fighters put on masks to protect them from smoke. These brave fire fighters rush into the burning building. They need to see if anyone is trapped inside.

Even fire fighters go to classes.

Fire fighters keep busy even when they are not fighting a fire. On some days, fire fighters have special classes. They learn to use new equipment. They practice their skills. They must not make mistakes when they are fighting a fire!

---

equipment: tools needed to do a job

What would you like to learn from a fire fighter?

Some fire fighters have a very special job. They visit schools to teach fire safety. They tell children how to prevent fires and how to report them. They teach children how to escape from a fire. They make sure schools are safe.

fire truck

Most fire fighters stay at the fire station for 24 hours—a full day and night. They eat and sleep there.

Fire fighters have chores at the fire station. They keep the station clean. They wash the fire trucks. They make sure the hoses and other tools work well. They keep themselves safe.

Fire fighters eat in the fire station. They make their meals. Some fire fighters shop for the food. Some cook. Others clean up and wash the dishes. Everyone helps, and everyone is glad when it is time to sit down to eat.

pole

A fire fighter uses a pole to move down quickly.

But sometimes the alarm goes off just as the fire fighters sit down!

Then the fire fighters quickly jump up. They leave their food on the table and rush off to fight another fire.

Fire fighters are busy all the time.